I strip my soul naked,
Words breathing life on paper,
A sanity in question,
Who is she you say?
Nobody.
A nobody of love,
The unbreakable,
Fearless kind.

LOVE and SHADOWS

Lida Dela

AUSTIN MACAULEY PUBLISHERS™
LONDON · CAMBRIDGE · NEW YORK · SHARJAH

Copyright © Lida Dela 2024

All rights reserved. No part of this publication may be reproduced, distributed, or transmitted in any form or by any means, including photocopying, recording, or other electronic or mechanical methods, without the prior written permission of the publisher, except in the case of brief quotations embodied in critical reviews and certain other non-commercial uses permitted by copyright law. For permission requests, write to the publisher.

Any person who commits any unauthorized act in relation to this publication may be liable to criminal prosecution and civil claims for damages.

Ordering Information
Quantity sales: Special discounts are available on quantity purchases by corporations, associations, and others. For details, contact the publisher at the address below.

Publisher's Cataloging-in-Publication data
Dela, Lida
Love and Shadows

ISBN 9781649790194 (Paperback)
ISBN 9781649790217 (ePub e-book)

Library of Congress Control Number: 2023900465

www.austinmacauley.com/us

First Published 2024
Austin Macauley Publishers LLC
40 Wall Street, 33rd Floor, Suite 3302
New York, NY 10005
USA

mail-usa@austinmacauley.com
+1 (646) 5125767

*Remind me, old friend,
Of what it was like,
Long before this,
When you and I did not exist,
When the white clouds heaped and
Never separated,
When roads did not cross for only
A moment in time,
And when love never met
Loss.*

Oh, love,
I am not my silhouette,
In me lies seas of the infinite love,
How can I not ponder on the grandness of it all?
I am not yet ready to be given a shroud.

What is it you fear, my love,
When you stare into my eyes.
When the ocean in yours meets
The heart in mine,
My silent presence
Piercing your soul,
A moment of hesitation,
An eternal pause,
You run
You hide
But why
Fear
Love?

She is far now, roaming the world,
I know you feel it too,
Your mind wonders…
Where has she gone?
There are not many answers except that there,
Solitude meets peace
And in that valley,
She does not want to leave.

*By the glistening dark skies
And the celestial winds,
Did you think it was me who was lost
When I chose to sacrifice my all for love,
And I see prism lights after storms turn souls into gold
And I call you in the night,
In rendered states of whispered prayers,
"Come,"
Eternity awaits.*

The signs of the divine are in the heavens and the Earth,
From the dirt beneath your feet to the stars above your head
From the whistling wind that blows wherever it wishes
And lifts the birds up to soar
Against the sky's caresses, from the beasts that roam freely Upon the green earth to the 'love-you'
Feel inside your chest.

*There was a kind of light in your eyes that
I saw in no one Else before,
Full of love, mercy, and hope,
It sparked love in the hearts of all those it
touched with just One look.*

The fog rises and lifts away; all begin to awake,
Birds glide in straight succession
Upon the lake—to take flight into a new day,
Deer's plowing through the hills, squirrels
Emerging from the bellies they create, all singing to their
Own songs, creating a heavenly choir that calms the heart.

Dear friend,
I will leave the key on the mat by the door,
Come whenever you like,
When your ship wrecks, when the only thing left to drink Are salty, bitter drinks,
When you have lost your way on the road for too long,
Come inside mine, in my house, in my home,
You will find safety here, a place
Where I will make my own yours.
Where I will help you heal those cracks that caused your Ship to sink,
Here, you will drink only the sweetest water and quench Your thirst with me.

Dear friend,
Do you see me standing here
As this life is fleeting by,
I often wonder about you,
Do you see me calling you through my prayers?
Do you hear me say 'I miss you'?
You are never too far from my heart, but never
Too close either,
You are a beautiful unsettling inside myself,
One that I will never let go of
And one that I will
Never forget.

Sit with me, here in this space,
I know you're not with me but in spirit,
Listen to that noise, the noise of stillness,
like the mornings
After storms cover the world with
blankets of snow,
There is only this moment
And for me, the world is quiet,
I cannot hear anything, not even the
pigeons by this lakeside I tread,
But only the sounds of your words singing
their tunes in my
Head.

Dear friend,
Do you remember those days?
We sat in the corner, tethered in blankets
of the warmest Days
Because we had known each other,
And we threw behind us a world where
souls caved into Desires,
And there was no more heartache and
Pain, when the world around us became
a frozen lake,
Would I dare plead for something
different?
Why nothing lasts forever?
The sun sets, the moon fades, the roses
wither away,
So, it is so,
That is life's way.

Walk with me into eternity,
So that even after the stars lose their luster
And the sun dies,
There will still be,
You and I.

There was a place I once belonged,
A place overseas,
Though I was too young
To remember,
The courses that changed
My destiny,
But still, I long to remember,
Of,
This time, this place,
There that I had been known
As me,
A young girl who was once loved
And accepted,
Before the tides,
Swept beneath her feet.

I'd like to be the only cascade of thoughts in your head,
Causing an avalanche in your heart,
My love slowly seeping in your veins,
Piercing every part of your being
Until the only thing you speak,
Is my name.

*I am sure of it,
That the stars love us,
More than them.*

Dear friend,
I almost lost myself again in all this world's nonsense;
Then I remembered today; how much I loved silence,
How it has always been my elixir,
Now I hold this holy book, this light, my lifelines, my Breath, my blood…
And everything just seems to make so much more
Sense again…

Hold me,
Like the moon holds the sun,
In the sacred circle of 'love'
Where there is no beginning or end
Just,
'Us'.

*I dream of greater things,
And you have planted the seeds in my heart,
If only it was as easy taking the high road as to fault,
But could we settle for the pond when there is a river to be Touched?
And if hope must live in our dreams, then let me keep Dreaming of the day when Rainbows will not leave us.*

Sometimes I wonder about your beauty,
How can something so broken,
Be so,
Lovely?

*I want to travel the galaxy with you,
Not just the world.*

Somewhere in the deep terrain of my heart,
There was you all along,
Your love echoed your
Sweet songs,
In a distance
Far off…
Yet,
So close
To
Mine.

Show me the poets
Those who have danced with the sun,
Show me those who
Have gone through the flames,
And still refuse to burn others,
Those are the ones
I believe
In.

I swallow my pride,
The pendulum swings,
The clock strikes relentlessly,
The test, the struggles,
Do I not bleed dark?
I am not the rock, the trees,
The flowers you see…
I am inharmoniously human
But still I think, Let me be holy,
Because today I know the price that
Comes when there is no love,
I will be the peace I need,
Amongst the trifling leaves and
Weeds of chaos,
I will be the breeze
Unmindful of the rhythmic dance
Of anything but love.

THE END